MY FIRST FOOTBALL HANDBOOK

Clive Gifford

KINGFISHER

Contents

What is football?	6	Passing the ball	18
Players and the pitch	8	Finding space	20
What to wear	10	Heading the ball	22
Ready to play	12	Shooting and scoring	24
Kick-off	14	Super skills	26
Under control	16	In training	28

MY FIRST FOOTBALL HANDBOOK

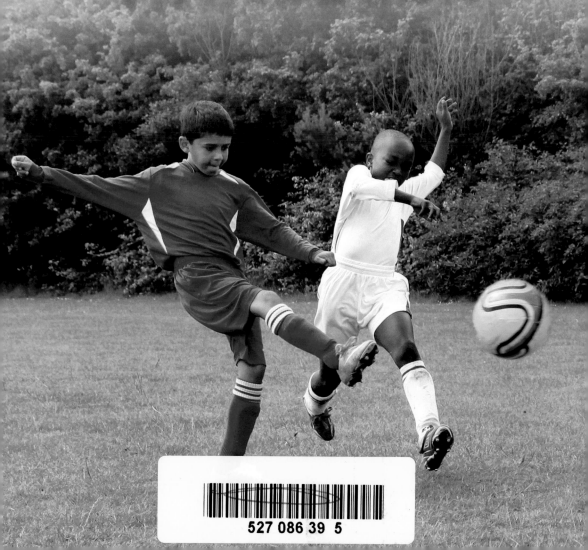

 KINGFISHER

First published 2012 by Kingfisher as *My First Football Book*
This revised edition published 2018 by Kingfisher
an imprint of Macmillan Children's Books
20 New Wharf Road, London N1 9RR
Associated companies throughout the world
www.panmacmillan.com

Copyright © Macmillan Publishers International Ltd 2012

Consultant: Jamie Fahey
Photographer: Michael Wicks

ISBN: 978-0-7534-4266-1

Printed in China
9 8 7 6 5 4 3 2 1
1TR/1017/WKT/UNTD/140MA

Note to readers: The website addresses listed in
this book are correct at the time of going to print.
However, due to the ever-changing nature of the
Internet, website addresses and content can change.
Websites can contain links that are unsuitable for
children. The publisher cannot be held responsible
for changes in website addresses or content or for
information obtained through third-party websites.
We strongly advise that Internet searches are
supervised by an adult.

Great save!	30	Top players	42
Playing in goal	32	At the match	44
Defending	34	Glossary	46
Tackling	36	Index and	
Meet the ref	38	acknowledgements	48
Free kicks and penalties	40		

What is football?

Football is an exciting, all-action team sport. A full match usually features two teams with 11 players each and lasts for 90 minutes. Young footballers often play shorter matches with fewer players in each team. Football demands great skill and fitness, but you will have to work together with your teammates to succeed.

An attacker shoots, kicking the ball hard towards the other team's goal.

boot

A player from the defending team tries to block the attacker's shot.

Over the line

For a goal to be scored, the whole of the football must cross the goal line between the two goal posts. The game is then re-started from the centre spot (see page 14). The team that scores the most goals wins the match!

Goal!

Football is all about goals. Goals win games. Players try to win possession of the football so that they can attack and score a goal. Players can run with the ball, pass it to a teammate or control the ball with their head, feet, legs or chest. Only the goalkeepers can use their hands or arms. The defending players try to win the ball back and stop their opponents from scoring a goal.

football

gloves

Goalkeepers can use any part of their body, including their hands and arms, to stop the ball going into the goal.

Players and the pitch

Football pitches vary in size. Full-size pitches are about 100 metres long and 70 metres wide. Most are covered with short grass although some have artificial turf. Full-size goals are 7.32 metres wide and 2.44 metres high. As a young player, you will probably play on smaller pitches with smaller goals.

Playing positions

A football team is made up of one goalkeeper and ten outfield players. If you are an outfield player, you will play in one of three positions – defender, midfielder or attacker. You and your teammates will line up in a pattern called a formation.

If you are a defender, you will try to keep the ball away from your goal by kicking or heading the ball clear.

If you are a goalkeeper, you can handle the ball inside your own penalty area. As a keeper, you can use your hands to make diving saves, catch the ball or to push or punch the ball away from your goal.

If you are a midfielder, you will need excellent all-round skills and you'll be good at attacking, passing and defending. You will have to be really fit as well, because you will run around a lot during a match.

As an attacker, you may play near the sidelines as a winger or in the middle of the pitch as a striker. A striker's job is to set up and score goals.

crossbar

goal post

goal area

centre circle

centre spot

sideline

halfway line

goal line

The pitch
Every pitch is divided into two halves with a goal at each end. A box called the penalty area surrounds each goal. The ball is in play when it is inside the boundary made by the sidelines and the goal lines. If the ball travels over a sideline, play stops and one team re-starts the match by taking a throw-in (see page 14).

penalty spot

penalty area

corner area

What to wear

All the players in a team wear the same coloured shirt, shorts and socks. This is called the team strip or kit. The one exception is the goalkeeper who wears a different coloured top, as well as gloves to grip the ball. Your boots are the most important part of your kit, and they will support your feet and ankles.

shirt

shorts

long socks

boots

Shinpads protect your shins and ankles from kicks. Make sure they are strapped on securely.

Neat and tidy

Tuck your shirt into your shorts and pull your socks up over your shinpads. Make sure you have removed any watches and jewellery before playing, as sharp edges could injure others.

water
bottle

You will sweat a lot when playing football. Make sure you drink water when training and playing.

Good fit
Your boots must fit really well because you will run a long distance during a match. Most boots are made of soft leather so that you can feel the ball when kicking it.

Boots
Boots have different soles so that they can grip different types of ground. Studs and blades are used to give you grip on muddy pitches. Some boots have small rubbery pimples for wearing on artificial pitches or hard ground.

Tie your boot laces tightly and tuck the ends firmly under the laces.

Ready to play

You have muscles all over your body and you will use most of them when you are running, tackling, shooting and heading. Always warm up and stretch your muscles before playing or training. This helps to stop injuries and allows your body to work at its best.

These players are running forwards and bringing their knees up to work really hard and get their heart beating faster.

Do some star jumps by leaping high and raising your arms. They are a great way to work all of your body.

Warm up

Some gentle jogging, skipping and running with your knees raised high are all good warm-up exercises. You can do them with teammates shortly before a training session or a match. They will help get the blood pumping round your body faster, ready for the action ahead.

Stretching

Young footballers learn how to stretch different muscles in their body, arms and legs. Stretches are always made slowly and smoothly. Never jerk or lunge into a stretch. Hold the stretch position for a few seconds before easing gently out of it. Always ask your coach if you are unsure how to do a stretch.

Your coach

Football coaches can show you a lot of things, including how to stretch well. Always listen to what they are saying and if you are unsure about anything, put your hand up and ask.

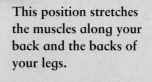

This position stretches the muscles along your back and the backs of your legs.

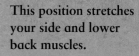

This position stretches your calf muscles at the back of your lower leg.

Lift and bend your heel back towards your bottom to stretch the muscles on the front of your thigh.

This position stretches your side and lower back muscles.

Kick-off

Every football match begins with a kick-off. It's an exciting, even nervous time as the game is about to start. Kick-offs are also used to re-start the match after a goal has been scored. The team who conceded the goal (let it in) gets the kick-off.

Throw-ins

A throw-in re-starts the game from where the ball crossed the sideline and left the pitch. Keep both hands on the ball and your feet on the ground during a throw-in, otherwise it is a foul throw and the throw-in will be re-taken by the other team.

1 Spread your hands around the back and sides of the ball. Take the ball back behind your head.

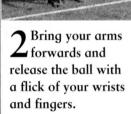

halfway line

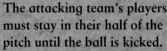

2 Bring your arms forwards and release the ball with a flick of your wrists and fingers.

The attacking team's players must stay in their half of the pitch until the ball is kicked.

Corners

Corners are given when a defender is the last player to touch the ball before it travels over the goal line. The ball must be placed in the corner area. It is then passed to a teammate nearby or crossed into the penalty area.

This corner taker runs up to the ball and strikes it towards the middle of the penalty area. His teammates will hope to head or shoot the ball towards goal.

ball on centre spot

The other team's players must not step into the attacking team's half until after the ball has been kicked.

The first touch of the ball at the kick-off must move the ball forwards into the other team's half of the pitch.

Back in the game

Top tip

As soon as you have taken a corner kick or throw-in, move back onto the pitch and look to get into space so that you can receive the ball back from a teammate.

Under control

A football game can be fast and the ball can fly towards you at lots of different speeds and angles. You can use different parts of your body to slow the ball down and bring it under control. Then you can make a pass, take a shot or move away with the ball.

1 To perform a thigh cushion, lift your knee as the ball drops towards you. The ball should land on the top of your thigh.

2 Drop your leg back and down as the ball arrives. This should kill the ball's speed and leave it on the floor in front of you.

Cushion the ball

Use the inside of your foot to control the ball when it races low across the ground. Draw your foot back as the ball arrives to slow it down.

This player gets his body over the ball as it arrives. He has turned his foot at the ankle so that the side of his foot meets the ball.

eyes
watching
ball

One touch

Your first touch does not have to cushion the ball. Instead, your first touch can be to pass the ball as soon as it arrives. This is called one-touch play.

his boy uses his est to control a igh ball. He holds is arms out for alance and leans ack as the ball rrives. The ball ill drop to his feet.

These two players are practising short one-touch passing. Each player has just one touch to steer the ball to the other player.

knees bent to elp balance

Control

Top tip

Here are some points to remember when controlling the ball:

• keep your eye on the ball

• get moving as soon as you have the ball under control

• practise controlling the ball with your chest, thighs and both of your feet as often as you can.

Passing the ball

Passing is an important skill and top footballers practise it every day. A series of good, accurate passes can move the ball up the pitch and create chances to score goals. Sloppy passing, though, can give the ball away to the other team.

Sidefoot pass
This pass uses the inside of your foot to strike the ball. It is the pass you will use the most often, especially over short distances. Practise your sidefoot passing as much as possible so that you can pass well with both feet.

2 With your body over the ball, strike the middle of the ball with the side of your foot.

1 Place your non-kicking foot beside the ball. Turn your kicking foot at the ankle as you swing your leg back and forwards smoothly.

On target

A good pass has to be aimed where the player receiving the ball wants it to go. When your teammates are moving around, this means aiming the ball a little ahead of them so that they can run onto the ball.

The ball is passed around an opponent. The receiver (left) is running forwards quickly, so the passer aims the ball well in front of her.

3 After hitting the ball, make sure your kicking foot keeps moving forwards. This is called the follow-through and it should point where you aimed your pass.

Passing drill

Practise passing as often as you can, with both feet and over shorter and longer distances. For a longer sidefoot pass, try to swing your foot back farther and strike firmly through the ball.

Finding space

Space on a football pitch is precious. If you are in some space, away from the other team's players, you may be in a great position to receive the ball. Space gives you time to control the ball, move with it and decide what to do next. Even if you do not have the ball, you should always look for space to move into.

1 The first player (left) has made a good pass to his teammate and then begins to sprint forwards past an opponent and into some space.

Spot space

Try to play football with your head up at all times. This allows you to look around the pitch and spot where the ball, players and space are on the pitch. If you spy a good space where a teammate can pass to you, move into it quickly.

Take a step and lean in one direction, then push off hard and sprint away in the opposite direction. This can trick the defender into heading the wrong way.

defender

Getting free

Players from the other team may try to stick close to you during a game. You need to get free in order to receive the ball. Try to change your speed and direction to shake off an opponent.

2 The second player passes the ball back to the first player, who runs onto the ball. This is a one-two pass – a simple way of using space to beat an opponent.

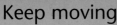

Keep moving

If you make a good run into some space but do not receive the ball, don't get disappointed and stand still. Move out of that space to leave it free for a teammate and try to find another space that you can move into.

A great way of practising how to find space and move into it is to play a small three against two game. The team of three tries to make as many passes as possible without losing possession.

Heading the ball

The ball can spend a lot of time in the air during a game, so all players need to learn how to head the ball well. Heading does not hurt, providing you keep your eyes open as long as you can. Try to watch the ball onto your forehead – the flattest and hardest part of your head.

You can build up your confidence by practising heading with a soft foam ball at first.

Standing or jumping

Sometimes you will be able to head the ball from a standing position. In this case, try to get your feet some distance apart to give you a firm, wide base. Much of the time, though, you will need to jump to reach the ball in the air.

Top tip

Clearing header

As you get better at heading, you can learn to use more or less force to head the ball different distances. To head the ball away from danger when defending, try to meet the ball at the top of your jump with lots of force. Aim through the middle and bottom of the ball to send it up and away a long distance.

1 Watch the ball as it comes towards you and get into position to time your jump upwards. You can hold your arms out to help your balance as you jump.

Heading practice

Like all football skills, lots and lots of practice will improve your heading. You can practise aiming your headers at small targets chalked up on a wall or work with a friend on getting your head over the ball to head it downwards. Heading down is useful when trying to score goals or directing the ball towards a teammate's feet.

In this practice drill, one player throws the ball up. The second player then heads it downwards so the first player can control the ball with his feet.

2 Spring up off of one foot to jump and meet the ball in mid-air. Pull your head and upper body back a little and keep your eyes on the ball.

3 Keep your neck muscles firm as you push your head and body forwards. Aim for your forehead to strike through the middle of the ball to send it flying away.

23

Shooting and scoring

You can think of shooting as passing the ball successfully into the goal, beating the goalkeeper and any defenders along the way. If you are close to goal, you can sometimes use a sidefoot pass to steer the ball into the goal. From farther away, you can strike the ball with your instep (where your boot laces are) to drive the ball powerfully.

1 To shoot using an instep drive, place your non-kicking foot beside the ball, toes pointing towards the target. Swing your kicking leg back.

2 Keep your head over the ball as you swing your leg forwards. Point your foot downwards and strike the centre of the ball with your boot laces.

3 Keep your foot pointing down as it swings firmly through the ball. Your leg should follow through, pointing towards the target.

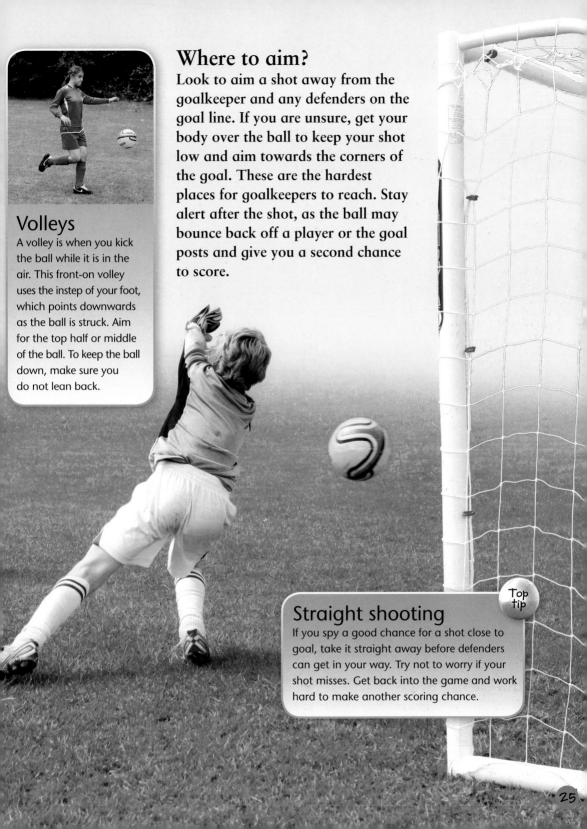

Volleys

A volley is when you kick the ball while it is in the air. This front-on volley uses the instep of your foot, which points downwards as the ball is struck. Aim for the top half or middle of the ball. To keep the ball down, make sure you do not lean back.

Where to aim?

Look to aim a shot away from the goalkeeper and any defenders on the goal line. If you are unsure, get your body over the ball to keep your shot low and aim towards the corners of the goal. These are the hardest places for goalkeepers to reach. Stay alert after the shot, as the ball may bounce back off a player or the goal posts and give you a second chance to score.

Top tip

Straight shooting

If you spy a good chance for a shot close to goal, take it straight away before defenders can get in your way. Try not to worry if your shot misses. Get back into the game and work hard to make another scoring chance.

Super skills

Passing and shooting are just two of the skills you can use on the pitch. Some other skills, such as running with the ball, can be risky near your own penalty area as you may lose the ball. Part of becoming a good footballer is knowing where and when to use certain skills.

Shielding the ball

As you receive the ball, stay aware of any opponents around you. One way of protecting the ball is to place your body between the ball and the opponent. Keep the ball under control as you move and look to pass or turn and run with it.

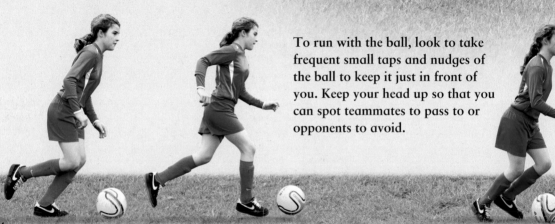

To run with the ball, look to take frequent small taps and nudges of the ball to keep it just in front of you. Keep your head up so that you can spot teammates to pass to or opponents to avoid.

Flicks, chips and tricks

There are many skills that you will only use now and then, but they are still good to learn. For example, a chip sends the ball high in the air. It can be used as a pass or to shoot the ball over a goalkeeper into the goal.

Chipping

You can practise chip passes with a friend by standing about ten paces in front of and behind a goal. Chip the ball so that it sails over the crossbar but lands as near as possible to your friend's feet.

Top tip

You can suddenly reverse the direction of the ball by rolling the sole of your boot over the top of the ball. This can work when a teammate is two or three paces behind you.

To make a chip, stab down sharply on the bottom of the ball with your foot pointed down. By doing this, you can send the ball up steeply into the air.

Outside flick

To make a quick, short pass to the side, twist your foot at the ankle sharply and flick the ball with the side of your boot. This is called a flick pass.

27

In training

Training is where you learn how to play with the rest of your team. During training sessions, you will practise many different football skills, with your coach helping. Training can be tiring work, with exercises to improve your speed and fitness. It is also an exciting chance to learn and improve and can be lots of fun.

The two players in white practise their close passing and moving in an area marked out by cones. The other two players in blue try to challenge for the ball to practise their defending skills.

These players are practising their close passing by making sure each sidefoot pass they make travels through the small hoops to reach their teammate.

Team tactics

Some of your training may focus on how your team attacks and defends at corners, throw-ins and free kicks. This is called set piece training. Your coach will teach you how the team should be organized in these situations and where you should position yourself.

Working with others

Apart from improving your individual skills, training allows you to see how your teammates play. You can learn how fast certain players can run and who is best at heading, shooting or tackling. This information is very useful in a big match.

You can work on keeping the ball under control with your feet by moving with the ball in and out of a row of cones. This can be turned into a fun race between two sets of players.

Top training

Treat a training session just as seriously as an important match and you will get more out of it. Listen to your coach's instructions, concentrate on each drill or game you take part in and always try your hardest. Training will make you a better footballer.

Top tip

To practise your shooting, put two cones on the goal line to divide the goal into three sections. Then pick a section to shoot at and see how many shots you can get on target.

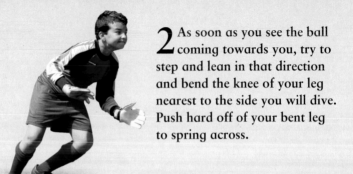

2 As soon as you see the ball coming towards you, try to step and lean in that direction and bend the knee of your leg nearest to the side you will dive. Push hard off of your bent leg to spring across.

1 Start in the ready position with your knees bent, your head level and eyes on the game ahead. Standing lightly on the balls of your feet, you should be ready to move or dive in any direction.

Palm away

If you cannot get both hands around the ball to catch it, look to deflect the ball around the goal post using the palms and fingers of your hands. Try never to push the ball back out in front of you as you may give an opponent a second chance to score.

Great save!

As the goalkeeper, you are your team's last line of defence. Sometimes you will be able to race out and catch the ball or kick it away to safety. At other times, though, you will need to be brave and make a diving save to stop the ball heading into your goal. Always keep your eyes on the ball in case it swerves or takes a sudden deflection.

pread your hands around
he sides and back of the ball.

4 Once you have a good grip
of the ball, gather it into
your body as quickly as you
can. This protects the ball as
you land on the ground.

3 As you dive, stretch
your arms out and a
ttle in front of you so
ou can watch the ball
ight into your hands.

Strike through the middle
of the ball firmly with
both fists to punch it
away a long distance.

Taking a high ball
f the ball sails high into your area,
ime your jump carefully and
tretch your arms up to catch
he ball above the heads of
ttackers from the other team.
f you cannot get both hands
ound the ball, you can
unch it away.

Playing in goal

There is much more to being a good goalkeeper than making stunning saves. Goalkeepers need to be able to concentrate on a game really hard as they may be called into action suddenly. They also need to be able to catch the ball securely, throw and kick the ball well and organize their defence.

To catch a ball at waist height, get your body behind the ball. Spread your hands and pull them into your body as the ball arrives.

To gather a low ball, get quickly in line with the path of the ball and drop to one knee. Scoop the ball up and into your chest to protect it.

Alert and aware

Watch the game and stay on the balls of your feet so you can move decisively. You can then react quickly to sudden situations, such as a quick pass from a teammate. In this case, you cannot pick the ball up, so you must kick the ball clear before an opponent reaches the ball or blocks your clearance.

A goalkeeper directs his defenders by shouting and pointing. A crowded penalty area can be a noisy place. So make your instructions short, clear and loud.

Distribution

Once the ball is in your hands, you need to throw or kick it out to get the game going again. This is called distribution. For shorter distances, you can roll the ball out using an underarm throw. Crouch low and bowl the ball out to your target.

In charge

As a goalkeeper, you are in charge of organizing a defence when the other team has a corner or free kick. You can also pass on warnings and advice throughout a game. Standing behind the rest of your team, you often have a great view of the game. This puts you in a good position to spot any problems, for example an opponent in space.

1 To perform a good kick, hold the ball out in front of you in both hands as you step forwards.

2 Drop the ball as you swing your leg back. You should aim to kick the ball just before it bounces.

3 Kick through the ball using your instep and let your leg follow through, pointing to the target.

Defending

When your team loses the ball, you need to defend to stop the other team from scoring and to try to regain the ball. Defending may not seem as much fun as attacking and scoring goals, but it is just as important. As soon as your team has won the ball back, you can turn defence into attack.

Working together

Every player in a team should be involved in defending. This includes the team's attackers, who can chase down the ball and try to force opponents into making mistakes. Players must work hard to reduce the amount of time and space the opposition has to play the ball.

The player in white does not have time to pass the ball to a teammate. Instead, she will kick the ball a long way up the pitch and away from her goal.

The two defenders in white are closing down the attacker in blue. One defender jockeys the attacker from behind, guiding him away from goal. The other defender is waiting for the right time to challenge the attacker and win the ball.

When marking, try to stay goalside (closer to your goal than the opponent) as you move with your opponent.

Marking

Marking is guarding a player from the other team closely as they move around the pitch. You move as the other player moves, trying to stop them from getting into space to receive the ball. If the player does receive the ball, you should be close enough to slow the attack and even put in a tackle.

Top tip

Safety first

Many goals are scored after a defender has won the ball but then dawdled and made a mistake. If you are under pressure from opponents, there is nothing wrong with kicking the ball out for a throw-in. Such a move will give you and your teammates a few precious seconds to get organized.

Tackling

If your team does not have the ball, you must try to win it back. Tackling is when you challenge directly for the ball. When tackling, always watch the ball and make sure your foot connects with it before you make any contact with the other player, otherwise you might commit a foul.

1 To make a front block tackle, keep your eyes on the ball as you step in with your knees bent a little.

Interception

Stay alert during a match and you may get the chance to intercept the ball. This happens when a player from the other team does not aim their pass very well or does not kick the ball with enough force. You may be able to nip in and reach the ball before the opponent.

The defender in white stretches to intercept the ball as it is passed between two opponents.

2 Get your weight over the foot you stand on as you make the tackle. Strike through the ball really firmly with the inside of your foot.

3 As the ball comes free, try to get it under control before moving away from your opponent.

Get there first

Sometimes, you and an opponent will compete for the ball at the same time. React quickly and try to get your body between your opponent and the ball to protect it.

Some shoulder contact is allowed when you and an opponent both chase after the ball at the same time. If you barge or push an opponent, however, the referee might award a free kick against you.

Top tip

Nudge away

If the opponent with the ball has his or her back to you, look for a chance to push the ball away. The ball may roll off the pitch or one of your team's players may be able to get to it first.

Meet the ref

A football match is run by a referee. There may also be two assistants who run up and down the pitch sidelines. They make many decisions throughout a match, such as which team gets a throw-in and whether or not a goal has been scored. You should always respect these decisions and never argue with the officials.

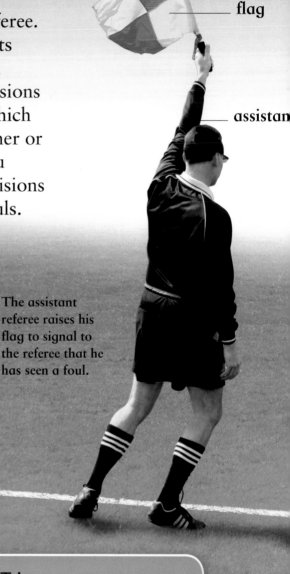

flag

assistan

Whistle blower

Each half of a match starts and ends with the referee blowing the whistle. In between, if you hear the referee's whistle, you must stop playing. The referee blows to stop the game for a number of reasons, including if a foul happens or if a player has a bad injury.

The assistant referee raises his flag to signal to the referee that he has seen a foul.

Trip
One player trips another during a W-League match in Australia. If the referee decides that the trip breaks the laws of the game, he will award a free kick. He may even show the player who committed the foul a card.

The defender in white is committing a foul by pulling the shirt of the opponent in blue to stop him moving.

The referee blows his whistle to stop the game. He may warn the player pulling the shirt and award a free kick (see page 40) to the other team.

(see page 40)

referee

whistle

Football fouls

Always try to play fairly and avoid making fouls like shirt-pulling. Other fouls include striking, kicking or jumping into an opponent or barging them to the ground. If a foul occurs, the referee is likely to stop the game and may warn or punish the player making the foul by showing them a yellow or red card.

Officials' signals

Throw-in

Substitution being made

Offside

Penalty

Indirect free kick

Corner

Goal kick

A yellow card is a warning to a player. Two yellows in the same match equal a red card.

A red card sees the player sent off the pitch and the player's team carry on with one player fewer.

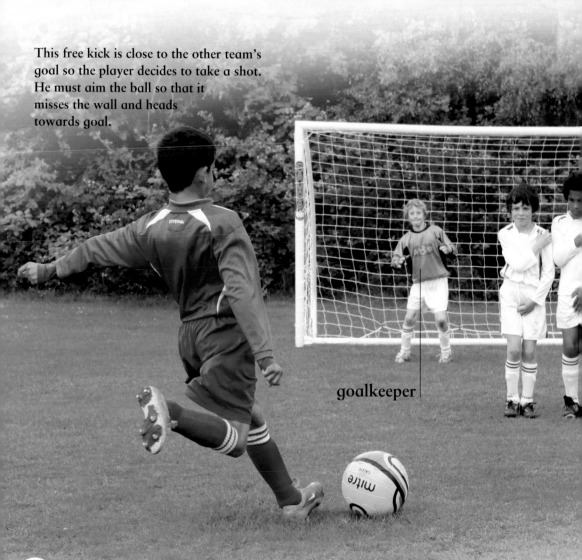

This free kick is close to the other team's goal so the player decides to take a shot. He must aim the ball so that it misses the wall and heads towards goal.

goalkeeper

Free kicks and penalties

A referee will often award a free kick to one team if a foul has occurred. On a full-size pitch, the other team's players must step back at least 9.1 metres from the ball, which is placed still on the ground. For serious fouls inside the penalty area, the referee will award a penalty, which is a really good chance to score a goal.

Penalty!

A penalty is taken from the penalty spot. Only the player taking the penalty and the other team's goalkeeper are allowed inside the penalty area until the ball is kicked. If taking a penalty, stay calm and make sure your shot is on target.

a wall of defenders tries to block the shot

Pass, shoot or cross?

A free kick near the other team's goal means you have to make a decision. Do you want to take a shot at goal or pass the ball to a teammate in a better position? If the free kick is to one side of the pitch, you might choose to cross the ball into the penalty area for a teammate to try to head or shoot towards goal.

You can pass the ball to the side at a free kick so that your teammate can have a clear shot at goal without the wall of defenders in the way.

Top players

Top footballers are professionals – it is their job to play for their club teams. The very best may also be picked for their country's national teams and may play at international tournaments such as the World Cup. Top players may take part in 50 or more games a year. They must be dedicated and look after their bodies to succeed.

Globetrotters

Brazilian midfielder Oscar (left) plays for Chinese club, SIPG Shanghai. He previously played for clubs in England, Italy and Brazil. Thousands of footballers play for clubs a long way away from their home country.

Harry Kane (right) leads Dele Ali (centre) and other members of the England team in a training exercise. Top players train almost every day to keep fit and sharp. They also work on their football skills throughout their career.

US attacker Carli Lloyd (centre) holds the Women's World Cup trophy after her team won the competition in 2015. Lloyd was voted the world's best female player in 2015 and 2016.

Injury

North Carolina Courage and Japan defender Yuri Kawamura walks on crutches in 2017 after she suffered a knee injury. Players have to work very hard to recover from injuries, some of which may stop them playing for months.

Brazil and PSG star Neymar signs a shirt for a fan. Top players are always in demand by fans and many make appearances to help charities.

Winning prizes

Famous players hope for glory and to win major competitions. They can also win personal awards. Cristiano Ronaldo won Euro 2016 with Portugal and the 2016 and 2017 Champions League with Real Madrid. He has also won the Ballon d'Or (golden ball) – awarded to the world's best footballer – four times.

At the match

Major football matches are colourful, noisy and exciting. Tens of thousands of fans crowd into a stadium, eager to see their heroes play and cheer their team on to what they hope will be an amazing victory. If you go to a match, watch closely how the players work together. See how they find and make space and how they defend and attack in groups. Most of all... enjoy the game!

Some spectators, such as this fan from Brazil, dress colourfully and paint their faces in the colours of the football team they support.

The Australia and Uzbekistan teams walk out onto a pitch before a game. They are accompanied by mascots – children chosen to walk out with the players.

France celebrates Antoine Griezmann scoring the winning goal against Germany at Euro 2016.

A match can see moments of drama or controversy. At the 2017 UEFA Champions League final, referee Felix Brych showed a red card to Juventus player Juan Cuandrado. Juventus lost to Real Madrid 4-1.

The coach

A coach picks the team that starts and can change the way it plays during the match. He or she can also change players by bringing on substitutes to replace tiring or struggling teammates. Here, Real Madrid coach Zinedine Zidane passes on instructions to Gareth Bale during an important match.

The final whistle

A match lasts 90 minutes, but time can be added on to allow for stoppages. Here, Croatia's Luka Modric (right) celebrates his team's win at Euro 2016 as the referee blows his whistle to end the game.

Glossary

Centre circle
A line 9.1 metres from the centre spot. At kick-off, the team without the ball must be outside the centre circle.

Chip
A pass or shot made by stabbing down onto the bottom of the ball to send it rising sharply into the air.

Clearance
When the defending team kicks or heads the ball away from danger.

Cross
Kicking the ball from near the sideline towards the penalty area.

Cushioning
Slowing a ball using your body, so that you get the ball under control.

Drill
An exercise performed to practise your skills.

Formation
The way a team's defenders, midfielders and attackers line up on the pitch.

Foul
An act by one of the players that breaks the rules. A foul may result in a free kick being awarded to the opposition.

Goal kick
A kick taken in the goal area after the ball has rolled over the goal line.

Handball
A type of foul when the ball is touched with the player's hand or arm.

Indirect free kick
A kick awarded by the referee that must be passed to another player before a shot at goal can be attempted.

Instep
The top of your football boot where the laces are.

Marking
A defensive skill where defenders guard an opponent to try to stop him getting the ball.

Opponent
A player from the team you are playing against.

Passing
Kicking or heading the ball to a teammate.

Penalty
A free kick taken from the penalty spot, which is awarded when a foul is committed in the penalty area.

Penalty area
The large box marked out on the pitch which surrounds a goal. Goalkeepers can handle the ball inside their penalty area.

Referee's assistants
The two officials in a match who run along the sidelines and help the referee run the game.

Shielding
The skill of placing your body between the ball and an opponent to protect the ball.

Substitute
A player who is brought into the game to replace a teammate who may be injured or getting tired.

Tackling
Using your foot to challenge for the ball and to attempt to win it from an opponent.

Throw-in
A way of re-starting the game after the ball has crossed the sideline.

Volley
When the football is kicked in mid-air by a player.

Wall
A line of defenders standing close together to protect their goal against a free kick.

Wall pass
A pair of passes between two players which sends the ball past a defender. Also known as a one-two.

For more information about learning football skills, attending coaching sessions and joining a junior football club, contact:

The Football Association
www.thefa.com/GetIntoFootball

The BBC's guide to football for children
www.bbc.co.uk/juniorfootball/

The new FA skills coaching centre
tescoskills.thefa.com/#Scene_1

Index

attacking 6, 8, 9
boots 6, 10, 11
cards 39, 45
catching the ball 31, 32
chests 17
chipping 27
clearing headers 22
close passing 28
coaches 13, 28, 43, 45
control 16–17, 20, 29
corners 15, 28, 33
cushioning the ball 16
defending 6, 8, 28, 34–35
distribution 33
diving saves 30–31
famous players 42–43
flick passes 27
follow-throughs 19
formations 8

fouls 36, 37, 38, 39
free kicks 28, 33, 38, 40–41
front block tackles 36–37
getting free 21
gloves 7, 10
goal kicks 33
goal lines 9, 15
goals 8
goalkeepers 7, 8, 10, 30–33
heading 8, 22–23
high balls 31
injuries 12, 38, 43
instep drives 24
interception 36
jumping headers 22–23
kick-off 14–15
kit 10

low balls 32
marking 21, 35
matches 44–45
midfielders 8, 9
officials' signals 39
one-touch play 17
one-two passes 21
passing 17, 18–19, 21
penalties 40, 41
penalty area 9, 15
pitches 8, 9
playing positions 8
punching the ball 31
receiving the ball 16–17, 20
referees 38–39
running with the ball 26
saves 30–31
scoring 7, 25
set pieces 28

shielding the ball 26
shinpads 10
shooting 24–25, 29
sidefoot passes 18, 24, 28
sidelines 9, 14, 38
skills 26–27, 42
space 20–21
star jumps 12
stretching 12, 13
tackling 36–37
team tactics 28
thigh cushion 16
throw-ins 9, 14, 15, 28, 35
training 12, 28–29, 42
volleys 25
warm-ups 12
whistles 38, 45

Acknowledgements

The publisher would like to thank the following for their help in the production of this book:

With special thanks to Jamie Fahey, Richard Close, Steve Pearse, Satwant Singh Brar, George Zadrozny and the boys and girls of Whiteknights FC: Benedict Bradley, Joe Close, Mattie Close, Fern Edgar, Conor Fahey, Dominic Fahey, Amir Idjer, Davis Lupindu, Dennis Medford, Jay Sharma-McLachlan, Mihir Shrivastava, Harjot Singh Brar, Stephen Walker-Boyd, Elsie Wood-Blagrove, Harvey Wood-Blagrove, Ammar Zulazman.

Created by Tall Tree Ltd
Cover design: Wildpixel Ltd
Photography: Michael Wicks

The publisher would like to thank the following for permission to reproduce their material. Every care has been taken to trace copyright holders.
Top = t; Bottom = b; Centre = c; Left = l; Right = r
38b Getty; 42t Getty/Masashi Hara/Stringer; 42b Getty/Dan Mullan; 43tl Getty/Lars Baron-FIFA; 43tr Getty/Icon Sportswire; 43bl Getty/ Vanderlei Almeida; 43br Getty/Gerard Julien; 44l Getty/AsiaPac; 44t Getty/Lars Baron; 44–45 Getty/Anne-Christine Poujoulat; 45tl Getty/Valerio Pennicino; 45tr Getty/Boris Streubel UEFA; 45br Getty/Francisco Leong.